W9-CMD-892

THE 100-YEAR-OLD CACTUS

THE
100-YEAR-OLD
CACTUS

by
ANITA HOLMES

illustrated by
CAROL LERNER

FOUR WINDS PRESS
New York

Author's Note

Research on desert plants and animals is ongoing, and many questions about these plants and animals remain unanswered. Young scientists should know, for example, that it is uncertain how long the Gila woodpecker waits to occupy a newly excavated nest, just as they should know that the lives of individual saguaros and woodpeckers will vary. This story offers one possible set of events.

10 9 8 7 6 5 4 3 2 1
The text of this book is set in 16 pt. Trump Mediaeval.
The illustrations are black line drawings with halftone overlays, prepared by the artist for black, green, and yellow.
Library of Congress Cataloging in Publication Data
Holmes, Anita.
The 100-year-old cactus.
Summary: Describes the first 100 years of the saguaro cactus as it grows from seed to adult plant in the hot, dry desert of Arizona and provides food and shelter for the desert animals.
1. Saguaro—Juvenile literature. 2. Saguaro—Ecology —Juvenile literature. 3. Desert ecology—Arizona— Juvenile literature. 4. Botany—Arizona—Ecology— Juvenile literature. [1. Saguaro. 2. Cactus. 3. Desert ecology. 4. Ecology] I. Lerner, Carol, ill. II. Title. III. Title: One-hundred-year-old cactus.
QK495.C11H53 1983 583'.47 82-21073
ISBN 0-590-07634-5

To
H. J. A.,
a devoted reader.
A. H.

To
JESSE,
a sometime
cactus enthusiast.
C. L.

This is the story of a giant cactus. It began to grow long before you or your parents were born. In fact, it started growing before people had cars or radios, and it may still be growing when you have children. The plant is called a *saguaro* (sa-WAH-ro).

The giant cactus lives in a hot, dry desert in Arizona. Only very hardy plants live here—and very hardy animals. You will find the names of some of these plants and animals in the pages of this story.

This saguaro was first a tiny black seed. The seed was no bigger than a grain of sand. It lay under a mesquite bush in the Arizona desert. It had lain there for a number of weeks. It had to have rain to begin growing.

One day in July, big black clouds moved in over the rocky desert mountains. They blotted out the hot desert sun and brought rain to the dry land. The dry desert soil soaked in some rain. The tiny cactus seed soaked in some rain, too. The seed swelled to twice its size.

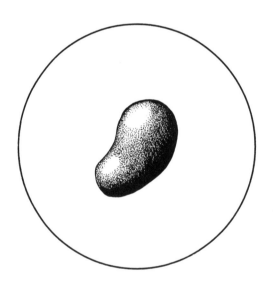

Sprouting seed

After the rainstorm, the sky cleared. The sun warmed the desert soil. It warmed the swollen seed. In a few days the tiny cactus seed opened. It sent a long, thin root into the ground. Then it sent two tiny seed leaves up through the desert soil. The little bush protected the tender cactus leaves from the burning sun.

One day a tiny green stem appeared between the two leaves. The stem was moist and succulent like the inside of a firm melon. Its tender green skin was covered with little spines to protect it.

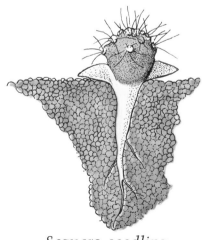

Saguaro seedling

Days and months and years went by. Each day was much like the day before. It did not rain very often. The little stem grew very slowly.

After one year the stem was no bigger than a kernel of corn.

After five years it was only one inch high.

After 15 years the plant had barely reached one foot. But it kept on growing.

At age 25 it was three feet.

At age 55 the cactus had reached 15 feet. Then it grew its first branch.

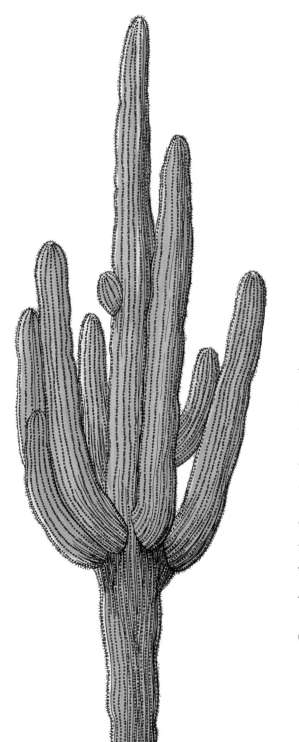

Now the cactus is about 100 years old. It is a strong, healthy adult plant. Its thick, moist trunk is about three feet around and 35 feet high—higher than a two-story building, higher than a telephone pole. It has seven thick branches and one round bud branch. One day the bud branch will be as big as the others.

Water is very scarce in the Arizona desert. The cactus has long, spreading roots to soak up water whenever it rains. The cactus lives on the water it stores in its spongy trunk and branches. Sometimes animals come to the cactus to find moisture.

Food and shade and places to live are also hard to find in the desert. A giant cactus can provide all these things for many animals.

It is spring in the rocky Arizona desert. The sky is bright and cloudless. The sun is shining hotly. A blanket of wild flowers covers the desert soil. Tiny green buds have popped up from the branches of the tall saguaro. They look like little green thumbs. Soon some will open into flowers.

These Gila woodpeckers are looking for a nesting place. They find the 100-year-old cactus. The male examines the saguaro's tall, thick trunk. It looks like a good place to build a deep nest.

The woodpecker begins pecking through the tough green skin. The stiff spines do not bother him. His mate helps. For several weeks the two birds chip away at the giant cactus. They get sticky and wet as they work building a narrow entrance and a deep room about the size of a small football.

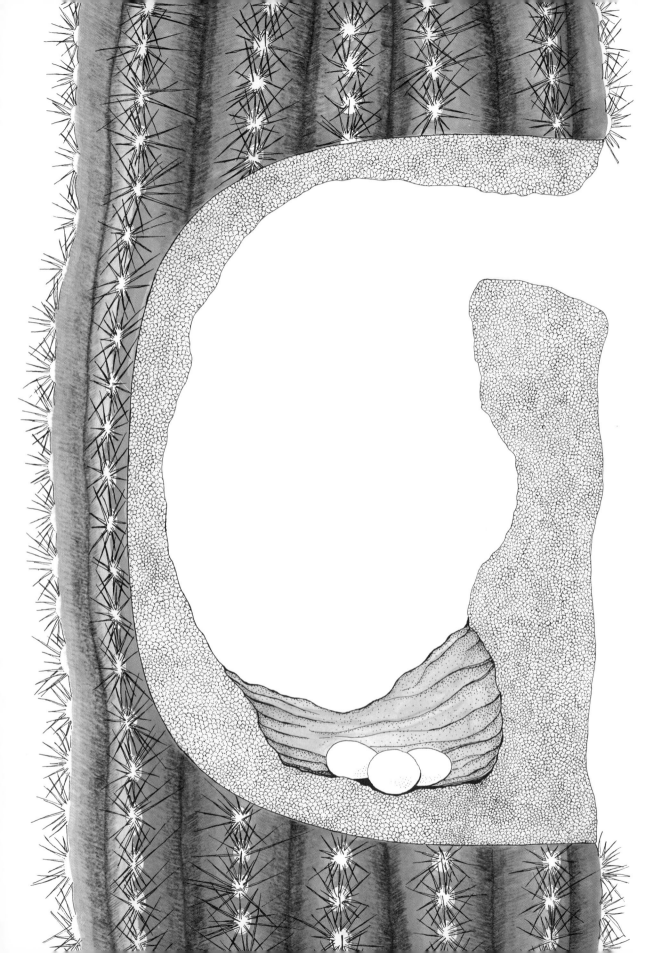

The birds wait until the walls of the deep nest begin to dry out. Then the female lays some white eggs at the bottom of the nest. The eggs will be safe in the giant cactus—safe from the burning sun, safe from hungry animals.

Another pair of woodpeckers, gilded flickers, comes to inspect the saguaro. The Gila woodpeckers chase the flickers away. The newcomers will have to find another saguaro in which to build a nest.

The tiny green buds of the saguaro are beginning to open. Now beautiful white flowers cover its high branches. The flowers are filled with nectar. The woodpeckers drink the sweet, sugary juice. Many other animals have come for a drink.

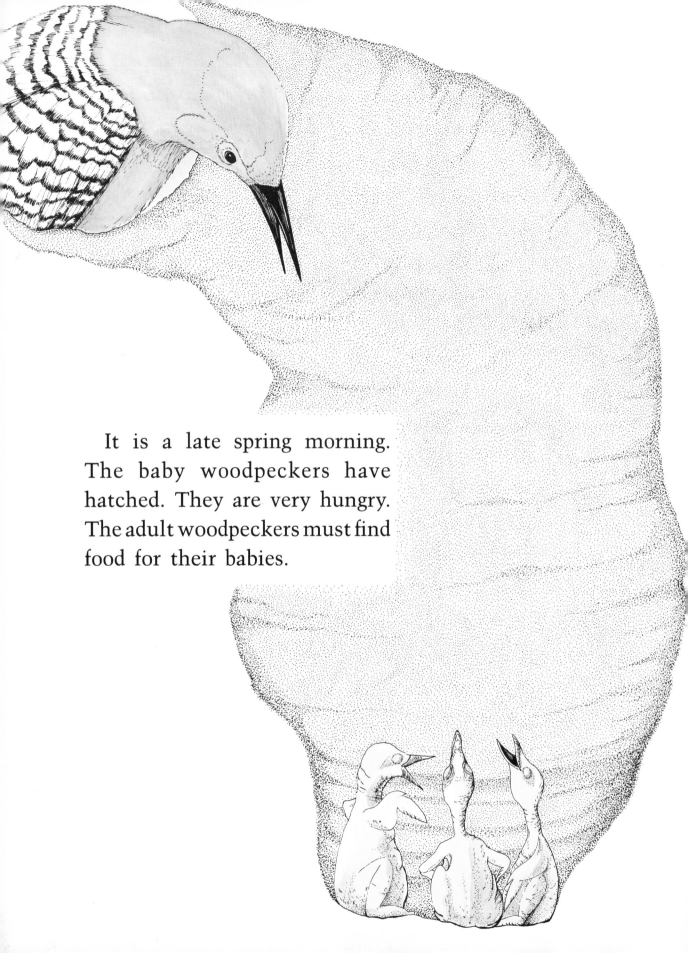

It is a late spring morning. The baby woodpeckers have hatched. They are very hungry. The adult woodpeckers must find food for their babies.

The woodpeckers hunt under the spines of the saguaro. They find a black beetle hiding there.

The birds search in the ribs of the cactus. Other crawling insects are hidden there.

Finally the woodpeckers peck in the unopened buds on top of the stems. Insects tunnel in the thumblike buds.

Night falls across the desert. The heavens are filled with thousands of stars. Tired from the day's activities, the bird family sleeps high in the cactus nest.

But not all the desert sleeps at night. Some animals come out after dark to look for food. Some come to sip nectar from the giant cactus flowers.

Some search on the ground beneath the cactus for things to eat.

The days of spring have slipped by one by one. Summer has arrived with temperatures over 100 degrees Fahrenheit almost every day.

The cactus flowers have withered and died. Now the saguaro is covered with green fruit. The meat inside the fruit is red and sweet and very juicy. It is filled with tiny black seeds. Many animals come to the cactus to eat the sweet red fruit.

The young woodpeckers have grown strong from eating fruit and insects. Now they are big and old enough to fly. It is time for them to leave their parents' nest. They fly off over the saguaros. Their parents leave the nest, too. Now that the young birds are gone, the nest is no longer needed.

It is quiet around the saguaro. The hole dug by the woodpeckers is empty. The 100-year-old cactus seems alone in the dry Arizona desert.

But wait. A young hawk is circling overhead. It is looking for a place to perch. Maybe it will find the branches of the very tall cactus.

Or perhaps a desert mouse will climb the saguaro's spiny trunk and find the dark wood-pecker hole. Many small desert creatures feel safe high up in a cactus.

A wide-eyed screech owl has found the saguaro. It will lay some eggs in the empty nest. By fall, the sounds of baby screech owls will be coming from within the giant cactus.

Year after year the saguaro will continue to grow. And year after year new animals will build nests in its trunk and find food and moisture in its high branches.

A 100-year-old cactus does not stand empty long!